A Shiksa's Guide to Shabbos:
Don't blow out the candles!

Helpful Tips for Blending In with Your Jewish Significant Other

MARCELLE SIRKUS

Copyright © 2018 Marcelle Sirkus. All rights reserved.
ISBN-13: 978-0692099698.

*Dedicated lovingly to Freddy Brand,
a mensch for all time.*

Always in my heart.

INTRODUCTION

What is a Shiksa?

[SHIK-zah = Jewish term for a non-Jewish woman]

Many will remember *Seinfeld*'s character Elaine discovering her "Shiks-appeal" in an episode in which Jewish men are practically throwing themselves at her, among them a Rabbi who pitches a proposal to whisk her away to a vacay in Myrtle Beach after the "high holidays."

During my (Jewish) husband's college years, he had a term for Jewish men who were attracted to non-Jewish women — he called them the "one in five's." He'd assert that one in five Jewish men partner up with a non-Jewish woman. There is no actual basis for the statistic, itself. And many years into our marriage, he'd revised it to "one in three," purely on personal observation.

I thought it was a silly statistic, and took no offense to it, perhaps because, for one thing, I'm Jewish, too!

So it would seem that we'd have smooth sailing when it came to deciding matters of religious observance in our home. But with my mostly non-observant background and non-existent Jewish education growing up, compared to my husband's conservative upbringing with many years spent as a member of an orthodox synagogue, I actually felt like a Shiksa. Over the years, I learned a lot about Judaism through our marriage.

The following pages highlight some well-known and many lesser-known holidays and traditions observed, along with a few lighthearted tips for getting through 'em.

So, enjoy the tips ahead, and let's party like it's 5759!
(That's "*1999*" in the Gregorian calendar . . . did you get it?!)

Tip #1
What kind of Yontif is today? Get a Jewish calendar.
[YAHN-tif = Holiday]

There's a lot more to know about the Jewish holidays than just Chanukah and Passover. In fact, there are more than 75 noteworthy Jewish holidays throughout the year, each with specific rules and rituals of observance.

Not only that, the holidays are observed according to the Jewish calendar, which aligns with the lunar cycles rather than the Gregorian — or civil — calendar, which is based on the sun.

It can be a tricky landscape to navigate, especially if you haven't been raised with these traditions and you are trying to blend in with your significant other's significant others.

A Jewish calendar will be very useful!

Tip #2
Don't blow out the Shabbos candles!
[SHAH-buhs = Yiddish term for the Jewish Sabbath]

Unlike the practice of blowing out candles, say, at a birthday party, once the prayer has been recited over the Shabbos candles, they should be allowed to remain in place and burn completely.

My mother-in-law insists on leaving the burning candles in place at the center of the dining table, for the entire meal, during which they occasionally set napkins on fire and often burn the arm-hair of anyone brave enough to reach over them and across the table for a piece of *challah* (braided bread) during the meal. (It's a small price to pay to stay in *her* good graces!)

Tip #3
Happy New Year! It's September! (And it's Rosh Hashanah.)
[RUSH-uh-SHUN-uh = Jewish New Year Festival]

Rosh Hashanah, which literally means "beginning of the year," is celebrated over a period of two days filled with festive meals, often including apples dipped in honey to symbolize wishes for a "sweet" upcoming year.

Rosh Hashanah officially kicks off the period known as the "High Holy Days" or "High Holidays."

Ten days after the beginning of Rosh Hashanah, a solemn time of reflection and penitence is observed, with personal reflection, and repentance for transgressions during the previous year, thus wiping the slate clean for the year ahead.

So, party now — and pay later — 'cause the next holiday on the calendar is Yom Kippur, the Day of Atonement!

Tip #4
No food or drinks are allowed in Temple during Yom Kippur.
[YUM-ki-POOR or sometimes yum-KIP-er = Day of Atonement]

If you are planning to attend a religious service on Yom Kippur, prepare to go without: no food, no beverages, no water. Nada. All day.

If you keep a nutrition bar in your purse for emergency situations, this is *not* the time to whip it out. Keep it under wraps!

Bonus Tip: The wearing of leather shoes is prohibited during Yom Kippur. Opt for rubber-soled shoes like sneakers, or athletic shoes. *Shoes* wisely!

Tip #5
It's Sukkot. You'll need a coat!
[soo-COAT = Jewish festival held in autumn]

For the entire week you may be dwelling, or at the very least *dining*, al fresco.

Sukkot is celebrated by living in (or for many, just eating your meals inside of) a tent-like shelter called a *sukkah*, built outdoors, to commemorate the sheltering of the Israelites in the wilderness.

During the fall season, for seven days and nights, all meals may be eaten inside of the sukkah.

The small structures are built under the open sky, made up of at least three walls under a roof typically made out of bamboo or palm tree branches. Cozy and drafty! Dress accordingly.

Tip #6
When is Chanukah this year?
[HAN-u-kah = Eight-Day Holiday, Festival of Lights]

If someone asked you "Hey, when is Christmas this year?" you would think the question was absurd. Of course you'd say, "It will be December 25th, same as it's been every year for the past 1600-plus years."

Chanukah, alternatively spelled *Hannukah*, and sometimes *Hanukkah* or *Channukah*, is celebrated during the Jewish month of *Kislev* on the Jewish calendar. Expect this eight-day celebration to shift Gregorian-calendar dates each year.

In 2016, the eve of the first day of Chanukah began on December 24.

In 2017, Chanukah eve began on December 12.

In 2018, it will begin on December 2.

You get the idea.

Tip #7
Tu B'Shevat. *Vat's* it all about?
[Too-beh-SHVAT = Jewish holiday honoring the new year of the trees]

Tu B'Shevat, or *Tu B'Shvat* or sometimes spelled *Tu BiShvat*, is a celebration of the "New Year" for the trees, marking the beginning of the earliest blooming trees in Israel at the start of their fruit-bearing cycle.

The day is celebrated by eating lots of fruit, especially those noted in the Torah — including figs, pomegranates, grapes, olives, and dates.

Another good way to celebrate is to plant a new tree!

Tip #8
Purim is *not* Jewish Halloween.
[POUR-um = Celebration to commemorate the defeat of Haman]

Purim is a joyful celebration held in the spring, usually coinciding with days in February and March, to commemorate the defeat of Haman's plot against the Jews as recorded in the book of Esther.

It is widely believed that the traditions of dressing in costume during this holiday may be traced back to Italian Jews during the 13th century who were taking cues from the celebrations happening at about the same time of the year in Italy leading up to the Catholic observance of Lent.

Purim is celebrated with a lively festival, wacky get-ups, traditional *hamantaschen* cookies, and plenty of wine! So Purim, and keep 'em coming!

Tip #9
Don't bring bread to a Passover Seder.
[SAY-d'r = Family home ritual as part of the Passover observance]

Passover is celebrated over a period of seven days to commemorate the exodus from Egyptian bondage. When breaking bread at Passover you will find that actual bread is definitely *not* welcomed to the soiree.

Instead, expect lots of matzah and baked goods made without leavening agents.

The traditional Seder meal includes readings from the *Haggadah* (pronounced HAGA-dah), a traditional Jewish text that explores the biblical story of Exodus, and includes prayers and songs that may inspire extended discussions of these themes amongst those participating. So dinner may be delayed an hour, or two. Or more.

Bonus Tip: If you're planning to attend a traditional Seder evening meal, eat a big lunch beforehand!

Tip #10
To kiss, or not to kiss, the Mezuzah — that is the question.
[ma-ZU-zah = a small parchment inscribed with a Jewish prayer, affixed to a doorpost.]

A mezuzah affixed to the doorpost of a Jewish home symbolizes the inhabitant's connection to the Jewish faith. It symbolizes one's connection to the Almighty when inside or outside of the dwelling.

When passing through the doorway, some people touch the mezuzah, and then kiss their fingertips. The kissing part is a relatively new tradition, introduced sometime around the sixteenth century.

You may choose to touch the mezuzah, touch and kiss, or do nothing at all. It's perfectly acceptable to opt out altogether.

Tip #11
Torah, torah, torah!
[TOR-ah = the first five books of the Hebrew Scriptures, also known as "The Book of the Law of Moses"]

During religious services in a synagogue (also called "temple") you may see that congregants are offered an opportunity to touch and kiss the Torah scroll. If you are not moved to participate, it's totally cool. But if you choose to kiss, be sure to do it the right way.

It's best *not* to kiss your fingers first and then touch your fingers to the Torah. (Imagine the decades of lip gloss that might accumulate on the sacred scroll if done this way!)

A better way to do this is to 1) touch the Torah first, then bring your fingers to your lips for the kiss, or 2) touch the Torah using a book, or some other instrument, then bring that item to your waiting pucker. No need to feel left out, if you opt out.

It's perfectly acceptable to let the Torah pass by sans smooch.

Tip #12
Holy two sets of Kosher dishes, Batman!
[KO-shurr = food prepared in accordance with Jewish law]

The word *kosher* means "pure" or "suitable," meaning fit for consumption.

There are many rules that govern a traditional kosher kitchen and kosher food preparation. And even more varying degrees by which many practice these rules, depending on their personal level of religious observance and interpretation.

There are rules for how some foods may be grown, harvested and prepared, as well as when they may be eaten. An example of this is the guideline for keeping milk and meat products separate, not to be eaten together in any combination or within the same meal.

The very religious often maintain two sets of dishes and utensils — one set used exclusively for foods containing milk and dairy products, and a separate set for meat products. It took yours truly nearly ten years to figure out which dishes, forks, spoons, and glasses to use when dining at my mother-in-law's home. If you're not sure, best to ask the host to provide what you need, rather than playing the guessing game.

Tip #13
Chai, how ya doing?
[KHAI, or pronounced like the word "High" = Hebrew word and symbol that means "life," "alive," or "living"]

The Hebrew word and symbol *chai* means "life." Chai is usually pronounced like the English word "hi" or "high."

"*L'Chaim*" in Hebrew is a popular toast meaning "to life." And while there is nothing particularly unique about clinking cocktail glasses together and shouting in good cheer, there is in fact quite a lot of historical relevance and tradition in the declaration itself.

According to the Talmud — the text of Jewish civil and ceremonial law dating back to at least the 5th century AD — when a drink is shared between two people it brings them closer together in camaraderie, and promotes good will for one another, as they wish for each other "a good life."

To that I say, "L'Chaim!"

Tip #14
Kippah, keepin' on.
[KEE-pa or sometimes kee-PA = skullcap traditionally worn by Jewish males in the synagogue, or any males attending religious services in a synagogue]

The kippah, perhaps better known as a *yarmulke* (pronounced YA-mah-kah) is most often worn by Jewish and non-Jewish men alike when in a synagogue during religious services. The very religious wear them nearly all the time.

And while they certainly satisfy Jewish law, they appear to defy the laws of gravity. Do they stay in place? They appear to. Do they ever fall off? Yes, actually they do — a lot.

Securing one in place is an easy fix with the use of a bobby pin or hair pin. In a pinch, a binder clip or even a paper clip will do the trick.

Tip #15
Hamsa on rye? No, definitely not.
[HAHM-za = ancient amulet symbolizing happiness, luck, health, and good fortune]

There are many variations of the spelling of hamsa, including among them *hamesh*, *chamsa*, and *khamsa*.

The hamsa hand is a familiar image across many religions. The hamsa, originally appearing in Middle Eastern cultures, symbolizes the Hand of God and is a protective sign for all faiths that recognize the symbol.

In more recent history, the hamsa has become a familiar symbol for Jewish people throughout the world, and has become an important symbol in Jewish art.

It is believed that the hamsa hand will bring its owner health, happiness, luck, good fortune, and protection. When the hand is facing downward, it is also believed to bring fertility and fulfillment of wishes. So, if you've got a special wish, talk to the hand!

Tip #16
Shofar as the eye can see, and ears can hear!
[SHOW-far = ancient musical instrument made out of a ram's horn, used during religious ceremonies; also pronounced like "chauffeur"]

The shofar is a familiar sight and sound at religious services throughout the year. It is most prominently featured when it is sounded at Rosh Hashanah and Yom Kippur.

There are many interpretations of the sounding of the shofar horn:
- the blowing of the ram's horn is analogous to the trumpets sounded at the coronation of kings throughout the ages
- it is a reminder of the destruction of the Temple in Jerusalem
- the sound calls us to feel humility as we exist in a manifested world supported by the Almighty
- the reverberation is a wake-up call at the start of the Rosh Hashanah holiday to begin our reflection for the ten-day period of penitence

And for yours truly, it is a welcome sound at the end of Yom Kippur services, when in my own interpretation the trumpet calls out, "Time to eat! Yom Kippur is over!"

Tip #17
Tefillin the blank.
[ta-FILL-in = cubic black leather boxes with leather straps that Orthodox Jewish men wear on their head and their arm during weekday morning prayer]

Tefillin is a religious article used during prayer by orthodox Jewish men. They are constructed of two small black leather boxes which contain verses from the Torah inscribed on parchment.

There are many biblical interpretations regarding "how to do it" and "why to do it." For many observant Jewish men, there are, no doubt, personal interpretations to go along with those.

This may very well be one of those practices that evoke from many, "Yeah, I'm Jewish, but I'm not *that* Jewish." That is an aspect of Judaism that I personally appreciate — one can do, or not do. Do what suits you best.

That said, my true purpose for including this not-so-commonly-seen practice (especially by the average shiksa, or a contemporary reformed Jew like myself) is that this page has served well "to fill in" the near-end of my book, which gets us to the final tip, #18, which you will see ends on a "chai" note!

Tip #18
Chai, again!

[HI, also sounds like the English word "High" = spelled the same as, and sounds like, *chai* as seen in Tip #13 in this book; noted here again but with an alternate meaning]

The Hebrew word *chai* is made up of two Hebrew letters, *chet* and *yud*, the eighth letter and the tenth letter of the Hebrew alphabet. Together, they add up to the number 18. It is widely acknowledged and accepted that the number 18 is therefore symbolic of *chai*, which means "life," and so it brings good luck.

There is a longstanding Jewish tradition of gifting, donating, or contributing in increments of $18, which then becomes not just a gift of money, but rather symbolically bestows upon the recipient the gift of a blessing for a good and long life.

It's not uncommon to give monetary gifts in multiples of $18, e.g., 2 x $18 = $36, 3 x $18 = $54, and notably ten times chai, (10 x $18 = $180) for an even bigger blessing!
And that is my 18th, and final tip.

So it is here at "chai," that we must now say, "good bye."

Hurray! You got to the end of the book. *Mazel tov*! (That means "congratulations"!)

ABOUT THE AUTHOR

MARCELLE SIRKUS

[SIR-kiss = author's maiden name of Eastern European origin. Pronounced like the word "circus." No relation to Barnum or Bailey]

Marcelle Sirkus is a writer and award-winning digital media producer living in Los Angeles, California, with her middle-school-aged son.

Suddenly and unexpectedly widowed in 2016 and left to raise her young son alone, she finds great comfort in the creative arts, and enjoys exploring the many projects she has inked over the past two years; they don't all pay the bills, but they feed her soul in a wonderful way.

Marcelle has promised her son that if this book sells more than 1,000 copies, she will get him a dog. Currently, they reside in a small condo apartment in a bustling part of the city. Moving a dog into their digs will likely require endless hours of city walking, chasing, washing, brushing, and caring for a pet that will probably pee and crap and shed and drool all over the place.

And though her son promises that he'll do his share of the pet-care responsibilities, Marcelle is pretty certain that he won't. So, if you are thinking about purchasing this book, please reconsider.*

Then again — maybe just go ahead and buy this book anyway! Marcelle promises, if you have Jewish loved ones in your life, it will come in handy!

*Secretly, Marcelle kinda wants a dog, too.

Illustrations

Illustrations for candle-blowing shiksa, smiling shiksa, calendar, and kosher-dishes by Daniel Naranjo.

Image credit "Apples and Honey" by Vector Toons
Image credit "No Food Allowed" by yumid/Shutterstock.com
Image credit "Sukkot Sukkah" by Liron Peer/Shutterstock.com
Image credit "Hanukah Menorah" by 9 Lives Illustration/Shutterstock.com
Image credit "Tu B'Shevat Tree" by iStock.com/rolandtopor
Image credit "Purim" by iStock.com/mementoil
Image credit "Passover Matzah" by iStock.com/olegtoka
Image credit "Mezuzah" by Slanapotam/Shutterstock.com
Image credit "Torah" by vectorOK/Shutterstock.com
Image credit "Chai #13" and "Chai #18" by Sharon Silverman Boyd/Shutterstock.com
Image credit "Kippah" by LAUDiseno/Shutterstock.com
Image credit "Hamsa" by Katika/Shutterstock.com
Image credit "Shofar" by illustratioz/Shutterstock.com
Image credit "Tefillin" by MasterGraph/Shutterstock.com
Image credit "Author Portrait" by caturchandra

Acknowledgments

A few people to thank . . .

First, I'd like to say "*Thanks, Mom!*" to my mom, Sandy Sirkus, for always encouraging my pursuits and creative endeavors, and for being my #1 one-woman cheer section!

I'd also like to thank Debbie Signer, my pal since junior high, for encouraging my silly ideas. Without her good humor and egging-me-on style, this book, along with many others, would probably still be buried away somewhere on my computer's hard drive in a folder lost in between thousands of digital photos and last year's tax returns.

Lastly, I'd like to thank my son, Jake, for his love, his die-hard persistence, and outstanding resilience that inspires me to strive for better every single day.

— MS

Copyright © 2018 Marcelle Sirkus. All rights reserved. ISBN-13: 978-0692099698.
No part of this book may be used or reproduced in any manner whatsoever without written permission from the publisher.

If you enjoyed "A Shiksa's Guide to Shabbos: Don't blow out the candles!" you might like the next book in this series, too!

A Shiksa's Guide to Jewish Cooking:
The secret ingredient is salt!

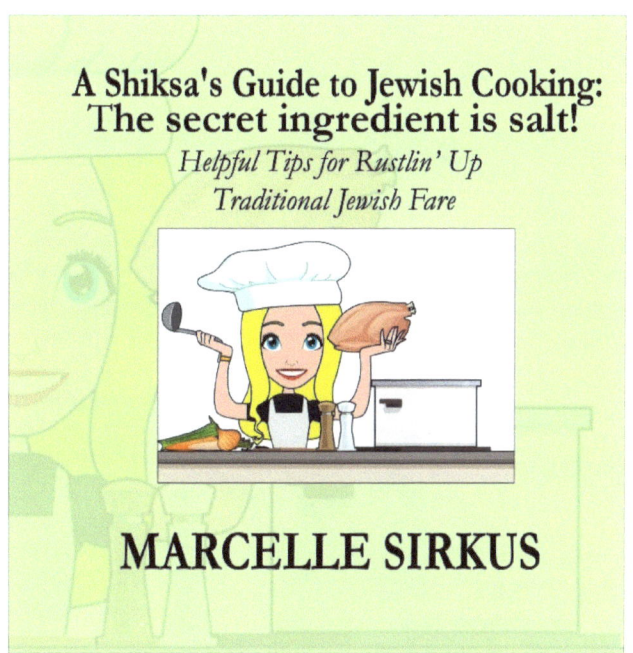

@shiksabooks   www.shiksabooks.com

www.ingramcontent.com/pod-product-compliance
Lightning Source LLC
Chambersburg PA
CBHW041540040426
42446CB00002B/177